More Reflections from a Former Evangelical

Poems Reminiscent of My 2020 Worldview*

Nicki Pappas

*subject to change as I do

Also by Nicki Pappas

As Familiar as Family: Leaving the Toxic Religion I Was Groomed For (2022)
*Reflections from a Former Evangelical: Poems Reminiscent of My 2019 Worldview** (2022)
Becoming Egalitarian: Our Journey from Hierarchy toward Mutuality (2023)

Inside You Will Find

About This Collection
of (More) Reflections

In April 2020, I participated in National Poetry Writing Month for the second year in a row. I'd joined the Fight Evil With Poetry Facebook group the year before and wrote a poem each day corresponding to the prompts that were provided. This collection, *More Reflections from a Former Evangelical*, contains the poetry I wrote in 2020. *More Reflections* is the second installment in a series of poetry books, with the first being *Reflections from a Former Evangelical*.

After self-publishing my memoir *As Familiar as Family* in 2022, I was looking for a way to fuse some joy back into my writing. That's why I released *Reflections from a Former Evangelical* soon after. In 2023, I self-published my second memoir, *Becoming Egalitarian*. It seemed fitting to revisit the next set of poems.

Each poem in *More Reflections* underwent some editing. Some were subject to a heavier hand of revision than others. The poems in Part A are my responses to a prompt a day from the Fight Evil With Poetry group. Those prompts are included so you can write your own responses if you'd like. The poems in Part B are some additional musings I wrote in 2020, as well as a few I found from 2019.

My hope for this poetry book is that it will motivate others who are on a similar journey as me to keep examining and re-examining once tightly held beliefs. I no longer worry that the words I enclose in this particular book (or any other book for that matter) will be irrelevant in the future. I figure at least some of them will be, and I think that's kind of the point. As a human, I am always processing new information and evolving. So, I honor the person I used to be while also holding myself accountable to continue healing and growing.

References to patriarchy, sexual trauma and violence, racism, homophobia, transphobia, and fatphobia, language that may be offensive to some readers, and abuse are present in the experiences included in these pages. Therefore, I want to encourage you to proceed with caution and take care of yourself. Thank you for holding space for me. As always, I'm sending so much love to you.

-Nicki

Part A.
A Prompt a Day

Dream Little One, Dream
April 1ˢᵗ prompt: write a poem about a childhood dream

In the front of my Lisa Frank diary
The first of my childhood dreams is recorded
It was March 6, 1998
When I penned the words
"To win a gold medal"

I have nothing shiny to point to
As an indication of this fantasy fulfilled
Not even a participation ribbon
But if I could do it all over again
I'd still tell little me to dream

Dear Future Nicki
April 2nd prompt: write a love poem to your future self

As Christina Aguilera sang in 2002
You are beautiful
In every single way

Don't despise those deeply etched lines
Encircling your sapphire eyes
They bear witness to years of laughter

Stop searching for gray hairs
To pluck from your scalp
They verify hard-won wisdom

Get comfortable with the stretch marks
Streaking across your stomach, breasts, and hips
They give evidence of the three humans you created

Embrace the pimples that often pepper your back
Without popping or concealing them
They reflect a fuller range of your humanity

Listen to each cue from your body
These nudges ensure your survival

Pay attention to your anger
It gives voice to a violated boundary

Draw your sadness near
Along with other exiled feelings

Keep leading your internal family
Into whole human flourishing
Future generations will thank you

Exchange the endless hustle for intentional rest
Your accomplishments don't determine your worth
You are loved and accepted just as you are

My Daily Comedic Relief
April 3rd prompt: write a poem about something funny

Maybe you have to be there
But I can't help but laugh
At the words coming out
Of my kids' mouths

Antimals and sockses
Once uponce a time
Cannonbunch for cannonball
When jumping in the pool

Crowns for crayons
Incessantly asking, "Please I?"
Yelling, "Where's pink bunny?"
At bedtime every single night

Minten for mint
"Pretend we're all different people"
One day when this house is quiet
I know I'll wish there was a sequel

Nicki Pappas

Mystery Can't Be Contained
April 4th prompt: write a poem about mystery

I once assumed divinity fit in a box
That I could tape shut, wrap, and decorate
But the tightly bound parcel popped open
And now all that really matters to me
Is becoming more at home with
Peeling away layers of mystery

Indispensable Parts

April 5th prompt: write a poem about a body

I was taught that the "Church"
Is one scattered body comprised
Of external and internal parts

Come sit at Ms. Donna's feet
Position yourself to deeply drink
From her fountain of wisdom
As she graciously speaks

Come pick up bags of clothes
From our neighbor Tianay's hands
Her tenderness and generosity
Are gifts to all who know her

Come be built up by single sisters
Danielle, Kari, Ruth, and Christine
As well as Sequana rapping
About LGBTQ+ inclusivity

Come gather around the table
Where the atmosphere Kate provides
Is sure to set even the most
Anxious at ease

Come let Danielle hold you
She'll be a refuge in the storm
While fervently expanding
Your view of God

Those deemed disposable
Are deeply indispensable
And to be part of a body
Is an invitation for healing
And wholeness in community

Nicki Pappas

The Importance of Schools
April 6th prompt: write a poem about education or learning

I saw in a Facebook post
That COVID-19 has shown
The public school system offers
Much more than an academic education

Questions abound during this time
Will we be able to maintain a routine?
How will students practice social skills?
What about those who aren't safe at home?
Who will care for them if their caregivers must work?
Where will the kids who suffer from food insecurity eat?

If public schools provide all of this and more
Why are there so many budget cuts?

When Keto Is Over
April 7th prompt: write a poem about food

My insurance provider said I'm overweight
The current digits on the scale
Mean we'll be paying more per month

So, I go on a Keto diet – again
I know the drill
If I want a snack
It must be high in fat
But I really miss carbs

Beginning April 20th
When my waistline
Is within the approved fatphobic range
I will indulge
In every sweet treat
Cupcakes
Milkshakes
Cinnamon rolls
Dr Pepper, too
Cookie dough ice cream
A glass of the most saccharine Moscato

My mouth will also feast
On the savory
Mac and cheese
French fries
Cresent rolls
Mashed potatoes
A burger *with* the brioche bun

Then, my blood sugar will crash – again
The room will spin
When I stand too swiftly
My appendages will go numb
While trembling and tingling

Getting my weight down
Will save us money
But at what cost?

Ryan O'Neal Sang It Best
April 8th prompt: write a poem about your favorite song

With my eyes closed on the bed
Sinking into Sleeping at Last's song
For Enneagram Threes
Makes salty teardrops
Trickle down my cheeks

My heart's desires displayed
In captivating melody and verse
To be seen, known, and loved
Appreciated and understood
Valued for who I am
Apart from what I do

Connecting with emotion
Setting healing into motion
Ripping off the masks
Resting from relentless tasks
Believing I truly am enough
And worthy of reciprocated love

Life Is Sweet
April 9th prompt: write a poem about a party you enjoyed

When I turned 30
It was dubbed the party of the century
(Okay, it was just dubbed that by me)
The colors were pink, gold, and mint green
The theme: Life is Sweet!

30 desserts in every variety
Moist red velvet cheesecake brownies
Made by my neighbor Tianay
Heart shaped Rice Krispie treats
And caramel shortbread
Prepared with love by Kate
Sugar cookies with the number 30 and est. 1989
Painted on the unyielding royal icing
Courtesy of Kari's culinary skills
Blueberry lemon cheesecake
Straight from Danielle's kitchen
White chocolate covered strawberries
Brownies and blondies
Doughnuts and doughnut holes
Banana pudding with chessmen butter cookies
White and milk chocolate chip cookies
Even oatmeal chocolate chip cookies
Cookie dough cheesecake
Strawberry cheesecake bites
Peanut butter cups and peanut butter pie
No bake peanut butter bars
Snickerdoodles
Oreo balls
Pecan pie tarts
Waffle cones with an ice cream bar
Root beer floats in Mason jars
Cupcakes and a vanilla cake
With homemade strawberry buttercream frosting
Adorned with gold sprinkles and pearls

Playing "How Well Do You Know
The Birthday Girl"

A small wooden chest full of gold wrapped candies
That I chunked at guests when they got a question correct
Poster board with pictures
To guess the year
A glass jar stuffed with memories
Of these beautiful people and me
Plus gold frames placed around the house
Displaying popular dessert puns
30 balloons in the living room
Props with a gold and pink photo booth
Singing "Happy Birthday" with sparklers
Under newly strung backyard lights
All of this on a rare kid-free night

My favorite part though
Was friends traveling
From near and far
Bringing tears to my eyes
And soothing my wounded heart
Proving that life is sweet indeed

Smoking Out Back

April 10th prompt: write a poem about a story a grandparent told you

If I've heard it once
I've heard it a thousand times
Grandma's story about the one time
She hung out clothes to dry on the line

Her bare feet lightly touched
The splintered back porch
She caught a whiff of smoke from cigarettes
My dad and his friends were the culprits

Rather than deal with their offense
She turned around and stepped back in
Letting the door slam behind
Signaling her impending arrival

With ample opportunity
To dispose of "cancer sticks"
My grandma rounded the corner
And all the boys evaded punishment

Courageous Confrontation
April 11th prompt: write a poem about a fear you've conquered

I was wracked with unabating anxiety
Toward the one who boasted spiritual authority
I courageously confronted him
Yet he never did repent
I now understand the absolute absurdity
Of the prerequisite of bravery
But I'm still proudly postured
When I think of this fear conquered

Inside My Four Paneled Walls
April 12th prompt: write a poem about your childhood bedroom

Step inside the weathered yellow trailer
Take eight steps through the kitchen
Make a left down the narrow hall
My bedroom is the first

Only large enough for my twin bed
A wooden dresser
And a bean bag chair
But temporarily big enough for me

A jewelry box
A diary that locks
Harry Potter books
In reading nooks

The tiniest closet
Stuffed with clothes
Sewn by Grandma
Or purchased by my aunts

Four paneled walls closing me in
I didn't know back then
That I'd soon grow up
And not want to look back again

Infectious Smiles
April 13th prompt: write a poem about something silly

We watched an episode of *100 Humans*
There was talk about tricking your mind
Into thinking you're happy by forming a smile
Stephen hasn't stopped grinning at me since

Monarchies Dismantled

April 14th prompt: write a poem about kings and queens

Down with monarchies
Return stolen lands
Move past the myth (and binary)
Of kind kings and queens
Embrace authentic community
Rooted in mutuality

Productivity
April 15th prompt: write a poem about your best feature

I get shit done
Yes, I intentionally rest
(More so now than I used to)
And I am no longer ashamed
Of the way I'm wired

When We Can Touch Again
April 16th prompt: write a poem about social distancing

I miss the warm embrace of sister friends
Here's a fair warning for when this ends
Brace yourself for uncomfortably long hugs

[As of January 2024, there are still COVID-19 variants of interest and variants that are being monitored. There are still surges of the virus and "hot spots" globally. I'm vaxxed and giving long hugs to those who consent, but I'm not sure if this will ever "end" like April 2020 Nicki expected.]

Faith Informed Wisdom

April 17th prompt: write a poem inspired by a quote you heard recently

Ekemini Uwan sent out a tweet
Of how faith and wisdom
Need not compete
Rather the former
Ought to inform the latter

It's been bouncing around
In the back of my mind
As I practice social distancing
During this time

I miss people and gatherings
But protecting the vulnerable
Is more important
And more like Jesus
Than arrogantly and ignorantly
Defying experts' orders

So, exercise faith all day
While wisely demonstrating
L-O-V-E
For your neighbor in this way

Legacy

April 18th prompt: write a poem about an important place

Legacy at Manchester Village
Is where my heart first skipped a beat
Waving him down on moving day
I had no idea my life would turn out this way

Walks at the park
Talks after dark
It felt like a romance
Right out of a novel

Almost twelve years later
We've been married a decade
Produced two mini-Steves and one mini-me
And we owe it all to that apartment building

History from the Margins
April 19th prompt: write a poem about history

I prefer history from the margins
For that is where the truer truth disrupts lies

Those who push and pull the levers of power
Are positioned to pen the present and the past
They revise and rewrite until they have a good edit
That positions them in a positive light
Constructing their truth that lies

They gain sympathizers
And fool broad audiences
Into believing things are as they say
Grasping for control to distort reality
But once protesters come on the scene
Ready to share the cut scenes
And what *really* went on behind the scenes
The original revisers cry out, "That's revisionist history!"
As they lie in wait for the opportune time
To smear the character of the suppressed
With lies, lies, lies

To prevent exposure of the scandal
They try to keep those they've subjugated ignorant
They confiscate and censor tools of communication
Discredit dissenters as being untrustworthy
They gaslight and deny
Though it's the oppressors that benefit
From a truth weaved from lies

I prefer history from the margins
For that is where the truer truth disrupts lies

The Double-Edged Nature of Mistakes
April 20th prompt: write a poem about a mistake

Had I not made that mistake
Who knows what path
I would have taken
I hate that it hurt someone else
And I can't guarantee the relationship
Would've ended naturally
Without me wounding her
And without altering
The trajectory of my life
That's the thing about mistakes
You can be riddled with guilt
Until your last day
But there's no telling
How much better
Or worse off you'd be
If you'd never "messed up"
In the first place

In the Rural South

April 21ˢᵗ prompt: write a poem about your culture

It's Sundays of fried chicken with mac and cheese
Corn on the cob and green beans
Sourdough bread fed with the same starter
Grandma has used for years

It's church three times a week
Revivals and Vacation Bible School
Special singing services and testimony
While filling up the baptismal pool

It's feuds of unremembered origins
Cover ups, scapegoats, and outcast sheep
Buried heads in scorching sand
To preserve a false sense of peace

It's the good, the bad, and the ugly
Patriarchy disguised as protection
And the lies of white supremacy
Enforcing gender and racial hierarchy

It's a selective mistrust of "big government"
An avoidance of the hospital and police
A "no one tells me what to do" attitude
And the isolating belief that family is all you need

It's "Don't forget where you came from"
As a tactic to guilt you into not leaving
When all you want is to spread your wings
Without hurting anyone's feelings

We Have the Money
April 22nd prompt: write a poem about an important social issue

On January 5, 2020
Donald Trump tweeted
"The United States just spent
Two Trillion Dollars on Military Equipment.
We are the biggest
And by far the BEST
In the World!
If Iran attacks an American Base,
Or any American,
We will be sending some of that brand new
Beautiful equipment their way…
And without hesitation."

Dr. Ibram X. Kendi's response was
"Two trillion dollars that can go to feeding,
Educating, and housing people —
Creating high-wage jobs,
Lifting folks economically,
Child care, slowing climate change,
Cultural projects, medical research,
And health care.
Don't ever believe the US
Doesn't have the money to help you."

Bastardization
April 23rd prompt: write a poem inspired by politics

The conflation of conservative politics
And white evangelical Christianity
Has created a deadly syncretic religion
With which the brown Jewish Jesus wouldn't identify

My Artistic Inspiration
April 24th prompt: write a poem inspired by a piece of visual art

For almost thirty years
I said I didn't have
An artistic bone in me
And believed it

But in December 2017
I put pen to paper
The first animal I drew
Was by Wendy of Draw So Cute
An orange and red lion
Full mane and bushy tail
Wide eyes with highlights inside

Simple step by step
Instructions to follow
Inspired nursery decor creation
And unique technique implementation
An entire line of framed photos
For family and friends

I'm not van Gogh, Picasso,
Or Leonardo da Vinci
But I don't have to be
Because there's only one me
Strengthening the artistic bones in my body

Your Name Here

April 25th prompt: write a poem about a name

What does your name say about you
Your lineage or loss of it
The dreams of those who chose it
Is your personality reflected
Is it something you've rejected
Do you give it much thought
Or do you rarely think about it at all
Would you change it if you could
If so, who would you become
If you exchanged one set
Of strung together letters
For another combination
Maybe you're completely content
And this linguistic exercise is meaningless
But one day you may wonder quietly
"What *does* my name say about me?"

I Just Wanna Write
April 26th prompt: write a poem about something you want

I'll you what I want
What I really, really want
Now you have "Wannabe" stuck in your head
You're welcome

But for real
I want to block off hours every day
To communicate convoluted thoughts
And simply write, write, write

COVID-19, Go Away
April 27th prompt: write a poem about COVID-19

COVID-19 go away
Don't come back
Any other day

This coronavirus disease
That originated in 2019
Is ruining 2020 for me

I acknowledge that many of my reasons
Are privileged and purely selfish
But 'the rona' really has me pissed

No yoga classes
No auditions or plays
No eating out at my favorite place

I hate wearing this mask
And constantly washing my hands
Though I do understand

My rigid standards won't bend
But I do miss hugging my friends
In desperation, I ask, "Will this ever end?"

The governor cancelling school for my oldest kid
While reopening businesses
Makes absolutely no sense

The death toll rises
We weren't prepared
Think of the lives that could've been spared

Lousy leadership continually incompetently exposed
45 talking about injecting disinfectant
Yet his base supports him even more

Sacrificing those perceived as weak
For the sake of our capitalistic economy
Is such dehumanizing ideology

If we'd sheltered globally
Simultaneously in February
We wouldn't be indoors now

COVID-19 go away
Don't come back
Any other day

You Can't Say You Didn't Know
April 28th prompt: write a poem inspired by freedom

How is it that someone can enjoy freedom
While others are oppressed to secure it
Especially once that someone is made aware

From chattel slavery to Black Codes
Through the era of Jim Crow
Until mass incarceration began
How is it that so many white folx
Remain unmoved by injustice

From the rape of enslaved women
Through public spectacle lynchings
Until modern acts of police brutality
How is it that large swaths of white folx
Remain unmoved by suffering

From the genocide of Indigenous groups
Through mortality of Black infants and mothers
Until COVID-19 death disparities
How is it that white folx
Remain unmoved by loss of life

How is it that someone can enjoy freedom
While others are oppressed to secure it
Especially once that someone is made aware

Remembering How to Play

April 29th prompt: write a poem inspired by nature

When I was younger
My brother and I used to
Spend afternoons after school
Scaling the bark of sturdy trees
Splashing in snake infested creeks
Storms didn't even deter us
We made capes from polyester sheets
Hoping they'd help as we took the leap off parked cars
In the woods, we spotted bald eagles and spotted fawns
We chased rabbits and deer across the front lawn
Grew corn stalks in the backyard
Then sprinted out to protect them when the hail fell

Now I'm thirty years old
And finally reconnecting with Mama Earth
Sprawled out in the dirt from which I was birthed
Grass blades prickling my arms and back
Clutching fresh green tufts in each hand
The sun toasts my pale skin that's peeking out
Then I'm entranced by a monarch butterfly
She leads the way to the woods
Wind whispers through the leaves
The branches beckon, "Come, beloved"
As I get in touch with my inner child
Little me demonstrates the proper technique
For indecently climbing trees
While I sing and laugh like I used to
When I was younger

Nicki Pappas

When Precipitation Falls

April 30th prompt: write a poem about the rain without using tired metaphors

I simply cannot sleep
When a storm is rolling through
I don't mind a drizzle
I'll even take a downpour
But there can be no trace of lightning
And not a single thunderclap

Drifting off while the water
Pelts my bedroom window
Is only peaceful for me
If I know for a fact
The house won't be crushed by a tree

As this is difficult to guarantee
It shouldn't be surprising
That I prefer to watch the rain
During the day while I'm awake

Part B.
Some Random Poems

I Want Magic
written: Aug. 30, 2019

The first streaks of light pour in
As morning is born of night
My inner turmoil is calmed
If only momentarily
I slowly inflate while breathing in
Then hold my breath and count
Before releasing every ounce of air
My stomach reminding me of the birthing ball
I've deflated at least three times

The stubble on my legs is highlighted
As the sun's rays dance across my skin
Exposing what I'm told are unflattering flaws
There's polish of a Caribbean blue popping
From toenails in need of another coat
Yet all I see is accented beauty
A blending of concealed and revealed
Mixing and messing with inherited categories

If there's anything I've learned
The past three decades
There's more magic in the mundane
Than I dared to believe
Hope, joy, and laughter
Overshadowing
Despair, sadness, and tears
If only momentarily

Time for a New Script
written: Sept. 2, 2019

Fawning as a response
To one abuser after another
Has been the case for me
Historically and presently

Fawning as a response
To one abuser after another
Has been the case for me
Historically and presently

Instability
written: Sept. 2, 2019

A common and shared enemy
Brings precarious proximity
To those who think
They have supremacy

Reveal It to Heal It
written: Sept. 2, 2019

Carrying undisclosed grief inside
Bottled up trauma hidden from everyone's eyes

Priorities
written: Oct. 24, 2019

Unread messages in Messenger
Texts that require a response
Overflowing Gmail inbox
A manipulative voicemail
From a virtual stranger
Social media and technology
Always demanding more from me
And I just want to sip coffee
While writing angsty poetry

Nicki Pappas

Extremes
written: Oct. 24, 2019

Oftentimes I'm insistent
That I'm at peace and content
Yet sometimes in an instant
I completely lose all my shit

Amorphicity
written: Oct. 24, 2019

Straight cis white men are not
The pinnacle of creation
Nor do they have the corner
On Divine image bearing

Nicki Pappas

Proximity Plus
written: Dec. 12, 2019

Coupled with proximity
I must have humility
If I'm to be changed
In relationships

No More
written: Dec. 14, 2019

Complementarian theology
Erases my humanity
As does every philosophy
That props up a hierarchy

Because of Beverly
written: July 14, 2020

"It was November 2016
I was set to cast a vote
For a third-party candidate
For the first time

But the longer I stood in that line
The more fearful I became
Though I didn't really know why
And I cast a vote for 45

It wasn't until May this year
I understood that this alignment
Communicated a lack of care
For my marginalized neighbors
But I care now
And aren't you so glad
That I'm no longer like them?"

Beverly tipped her head to the side
Before releasing the words
"Well, to care
Is literally the bare
Minimum
Also, *why* are you telling me this?"

Defensively I blurted out
"So, what, I shouldn't care?"

She locked eyes with me
As she stated emphatically
"You know
I'm not saying not to care
But don't be lulled into complacency
Thinking that as a newly minted
Liberal white woman who
Decided to care thirty years too late
That you somehow aren't still part
Of the problem

And that just because you are now awake
To the injustices Black people have *been* talking about
That you somehow know better than us
Regarding how to solve them
The arrogance
To believe yourself an expert in this
After mere months of researching
My lived experience
Gives evidence
Of the toxic whiteness
You still need to deal with
While you ask yourself
How much of your engagement
Is performative
It took you three decades to learn
The white lies you've internalized
What makes you think
You've uprooted it all already
My advice
Sit down
Listen
Read some books
Then read some more
And for the love of God
Stop positioning yourself
As an authority
For other white folx to look to"

It's been three years
And I'm still taking Beverly's advice
I stopped relaying the story
Of that day at the ballot box
As a form of penance
I ceased seeking absolution
I came out from under the delusion
That the recitation of my
"I'm a good white person" résumé
Should automatically put Black people at ease
Because what often matters more
Are the antiracism actions that no one sees
As I'm moving past the good/bad binary
I refuse to conceal who I used to be

In an effort to pretend
The problem still isn't me

In November 2016
I was set to cast a vote
For a third-party candidate
For the first time

But the longer I stood in that line
The more fearful I became
Now I know why
I chose the power
That comes from being white
And I cast a vote for 45

I told myself
I did it because of abortion
A convenient "moral" disguise
To cover up that I didn't
Actually care about Black lives

It's easier to hide behind
A hypothetical womb
Than to admit a lack of love
For babies when they grow up

Beverly taught me
That caring alone
Doesn't dismantle oppressive systems
Caring on its own
Does little to address centuries
Of unearned gain
That has privileged me
Again and again
Caring is insufficient
If not coupled with commitment
To structural change
And continual self-reflection
To examine how I still uphold
Institutional racism today

I am dedicated
To living justly
Under the leadership
Of every Beverly
Until she receives
Equal access and opportunity
Because I really believe
Beverly's well-being
Is the key
To whole human flourishing

[Certain aspects of this poem did take place, like me voting for 45 in 2016, but this is a fictionalized conversation. This poem is a compilation of years of conversations and of learning from various people like NC historian Lettie Gore, pleasure activist and author Tina Strawn, liberation educator Weeze, and so many others.]

Slow Down
written: Nov. 11, 2020

Micah Bournes said poets
Move through the world
A little slower
If I'm going to be a poet
Looks like I need
To slow down

Breathing in Beauty
written: Nov. 11, 2020

For the last poem I wrote
About Micah Bournes' words
I grabbed what I thought
Was a black pen

When the brown ink
Appeared on the page
I breathed in the beauty

I also found it funny
That just moments before
I wrote about slowing down
I was moving too quickly
To notice the color

Acknowledgements

I want to express my deep gratitude for every person who read *Reflections from a Former Evangelical,* the first installment in this collection of reflections. The support and feedback you all gave me provided the encouragement I needed to revisit more of my previous poetry and to pen new poems. Thank you!

Thank you for reading
More Reflections from a Former Evangelical:
Poems Reminiscent of My 2020 Worldview.
If you enjoyed this book, please share an
online review on Amazon and Goodreads.

KEEP IN TOUCH WITH NICKI PAPPAS

Website: nickipappas.com
Podcast: *Broadening the Narrative*
Instagram: @broadeningthenarrative
TikTok: @broadeningthenarrative
Twitter: @broadnarrative
Facebook: facebook.com/groups/
broadeningthenarrative